COPING

WITH

DYING

The Loss of a Loved One

George Seber

Published by DayStar Books Ltd
PO Box 65275, Mairangi Bay, Auckland 0754

ISBN: 978-0-995-11177-6 pbk
ISBN: 978-0-473-50509-7 epub

Production by Outline Print Consultancy
Ingram Spark 2019 international distribution
wildsidepublishing.com

Dedication

In memory of Peter Matthews –

a kind and gentle man who will be deeply missed.

Contents

PREFACE

There are two certain things in life – birth and death – and they create strong emotions in onlookers. There is an old saying about other certain things, such as taxes, but that five-letter word is more a source of irritation.

My first wife was diagnosed with breast cancer at 40 years of age and spent the next six years fighting it before it finally went to her bones. Those extra years of life, however, were very valuable for many reasons, not the least being all the things we were able to do as a family. It also enabled our two sons to grow older so that even though there was a major impact when she died, they had reached the ages eleven and fourteen and were therefore better able to cope.

After a period in hospital my wife wanted to die at home, which was a good idea. I managed to get leave from my university, where I was a professor of statistics, and looked after her for about five weeks. It was a marathon.

In the evening I would sit next to her as she read, which she liked to do, while I worked on writing a statistics book as a distraction. We did have a couple of nurses who helped her for a short period of time each day towards the end. It was not easy having to wake her every four hours to give her morphine, and this played havoc with my sleep. However, she was always a positive person and managed to survive until our 25th wedding anniversary, spending her last two days in a hospice.

It was a privilege to look after her. I also learned some useful housekeeping skills that stood me in good stead later.

Jumping ahead 33 years, having been remarried again for 26 of them, I have had three male friends die in the last twelve months, all around my age (80). One of them lived a two-hour flight away and his wife, a close friend of my wife, kept us informed as to how he was doing as we wanted to attend his funeral.

At the time I was writing up some notes about what we can expect when a person is near the end of his/her life. I trained to become a counsellor/psychotherapist and a supervisor and have now had almost sixteen years of counselling experience. I have written a large book on counselling, which contained a chapter on grief, but written for the counsellor and not the grieving person.

As we waited to fly to the funeral of my friend I decided I needed to write a booklet on the subject: about what happens when a person is dying an'd what it might be like recovering from the death of a loved one, as there is a paucity of information on these two topics. I have tried to cover a wide spectrum relating to death including dealing with sudden death from an accident or suicide, and the death of children.

It is hoped that this booklet will help the reader to better understand the whole process. We are, however, all different in how we respond to dying and death, so I have taken a broad-brush approach.

It is hoped that this booklet might be useful for doctors, nurses, hospice teams, pastors and counsellors; in fact, for anyone caring for a dying person or recovering from their death.

George A F Seber

January 2019

1

The Onset of Death

Introduction

In some cultures, such as that of New Zealand's white Kiwi, death is not often talked about. This can lead to a number of problems when a terminal illness turns up on the horizon.

The first is that adequate preparations may not be made, and loved ones left behind after a death can feel confused and overwhelmed about what needs to be done. Secondly, there may not be adequate communication between the patient and the family caregiver, so that the latter may not know what the former wants both physically and psychologically as they face the future together. This lack of appropriate communication can arise out of denial by both parties, who believe the patient will recover. Therefore, they put off talking about the end game. The opportunity can be lost if the loved one becomes unable to communicate properly.

In addition to this stress might be the feeling they did not say goodbye adequately. The situation is even worse if a loved one dies suddenly in an accident or commits suicide.

In the past people tended to die from infections and viruses, but with the advent of antibiotics and vaccinations some diseases have almost been eliminated. However, with the overuse of antibiotics combined with mutations of the beasties, we are still having problems with some bugs becoming resistant to antibiotics. Eight years ago I nearly died of a so-called "super-bug" MRSA (Methicillin-Resistant Staphylococcus Aureus). However, in spite of these rarer bugs, people today tend to fall ill from chronic (long-lasting) diseases such as heart disease, stroke, cancer, diabetes, obesity and arthritis; the period of these illnesses can be a lot longer. As people live longer, they may also become more prone to mental disorders such as dementia and Alzheimer's. This can lead to extended and at times difficult care that makes it much harder to plan ahead, which I now discuss.

Planning

Firstly, it is important to keep wills up to date in case of sudden death. Talking about death with your partner is not morbid or self-fulfilling, but commonsense. Wills can lead to a lot of family tension and sometimes dissension, so they need to be dealt with when a loved one is thinking clearly and rationally. These days, second and even third or more marriages are not uncommon, which often entails blended families with children belonging to both partners. In this case separate wills are needed as well as a combined will if both die at once (say, in an accident).

It is helpful to have in writing who gets what from the assets. For example, she may want a particular ring to go to a certain niece, or he a guitar to a particular nephew. If you are married, in a civil union partnership, or in a de facto relationship, you will be affected by the Property Relationships Act (the PRA) of 2002 if your partner dies. If there is no will or previous agreement the act presumes that each partner contributes equally to their relationship, even though that may be in different ways.

The act aims to provide a just division (almost always equal) of the relationship property. Usually a relationship will need to have lasted at least three years for the PRA's equal-sharing regime to apply. However, sometimes shorter relationships, where there are children involved or a partner has made a substantial contribution, will also qualify, if that would be just.

A relationship that has not lasted for three years is classified as a relationship of short duration and different principles are applied in dividing the property. For further details see Dividing up Relationship Property, New Zealand, on the Internet. If there are beginning signs of mental deterioration, setting up a POA (Power of Attorney) may be needed. If there is both a will and a PRA operating the survivor has a choice but cannot use both.

In preparing a will an executor or executors need to be nominated, and their responsibility is to ensure that the wishes of the deceased are carried out according to the will and any codicils that might get added. Usually one or more family members or a close friend are appointed, and the estate's lawyer can also provide help. However, if there isn't a suitable person capable of managing the estate a lawyer can be appointed as the executor, with certain legal obligations. If so, the cost will come out of the estate.

There is one other factor that needs to be considered before the death of a loved one. It is the question of what happens to a joint bank account after death. Logically, the account should be transferred to the surviving person so that money is readily available and bills paid, but there can be some problems with regard to such things as debts. Some banks freeze joint accounts until the issues of probate are resolved. I have heard of cases where the only bank account is a joint one, which has been frozen for some weeks, and the surviving person has had to borrow money to survive in the meantime.

The banks tend to view each case on its own merits; clear guidelines do not seem to be available. If the survivor has his/her own bank account he/she will have access to money, but not every partnership will have separate accounts for each partner as well as a joint account. At some stage it may be helpful to enquire from the bank as to their policy on this matter if the death of the loved one is immanent.

When families are involved decision-making can be difficult as they may be unable to make timely decisions that respect the patient's wishes and values. This can result in over-treatment, under-treatment, and other problems. For example, family members may differ over whether life extension or life quality is the main goal of treatment. They may demand common treatments such as antibiotics for pneumonia or drugs to reduce high blood pressure without wondering if that person might prefer dying quickly, rather than having a lengthy decline in a skilled care facility.

It is clear from the above discussion that there needs to be adequate planning. It is important to know what the patient wants. Some good ideas for planning are available on the Advance Care Planning website (http://www.advancecareplanning.org.nz), which I will summarise briefly with regard to what matters to the patient. Things to think about include the sort of care they might prefer, who would make decisions if the patient wasn't able to, and how/where they would like to spend their last days. If it's manageable, the first choice in the latter case is usually to be at home.

It is helpful for the patient to talk about these things with an appropriate person, and it is a good idea to write things down. As we never know when our time is up, especially as we get older, it is a good idea to do these things while life is normal and also decide who should have a copy. This can be reviewed from time to time, preferably at a fixed date each year.

If an illness is likely to be protracted, it not only provides an opportunity to deal with unfinished business but also enables us to rehearse in our minds how we will cope when our loved one has died, especially when children are involved. Some may be in denial on the grounds it is inappropriate to anticipate death in any way. If the illness is lengthy there can be problems with regard to the emotional distance between the dying person and concerned others. The dying person may withdraw because the process is so long and they want to prepare for the ultimate separation. Sometimes a carer may feel guilty for wanting it to end. On the other hand, people may get too close to the patient in order to try and compensate for their guilty feelings and ambivalence towards the dying person.

Dementia

A brief word about dementia. It is progressive and fatal, and may occur at the later stages of an illness. However, it should be noted that dementia is not a normal part of the ageing process, though it is more common for people over the age of 65, and can affect people as young as 45. Some older people may suffer from mild cognitive impairment that causes a slight but noticeable and measurable decline in cognitive abilities, including memory and thinking skills. Such a person is at an increased risk of developing Alzheimer's or dementia.

There are many causes of dementia, but the most common is Alzheimer's disease (60 to 80 percent of dementia patients) where there are tangles and a build-up of beta-amyloid proteins (plaque) in the brain, along with dying brain cells. Tangles are dense deposits of non-functional protein that are found on the outside of nerve cells, while plaques develop in the hippocampus and areas for memory, thinking and making decisions. Any damage to brain cells interferes with the ability of them to communicate with each other so that thinking, behaviour and feelings can be affected.

A person can have a combination of different causes of dementia and each cause tends to affect particular areas of the brain, leading to different changes in a person's behaviour. However, in the end symptoms become much the same, usually referred to as late-stage or advanced dementia. Such a person will have difficulties with daily activities like bathing, dressing, eating, and going to the bathroom. They may be unable to walk or even sit up without assistance. They can become bed-bound and require around-the-clock care.

What is difficult for the caregiver is that the loved one will also lose the ability to speak and make facial expressions, including the ability to smile. They also may not recognise people.

Losing the ability to move means that in the end a person in the late stage of dementia is at risk of a number of medical complications including infections of, for example, the urinary tract, or pneumonia from swallowing difficulties, that they are too weak to fight off.

I don't want to dwell too much on dementia as my focus is on the last days, but it is helpful to have a general idea of the symptoms, which are taken from Dr Sandra Cabot (2005) and are also available on the internet, for example, https://www.alz.org/what-is-dementia.asp.

Memory loss is one symptom, although mild forgetfulness and temporary loss of memory occurs in everyone, especially as we age. (What was I saying?) This can be due to depression – which often accompanies Alzheimer's – stress, ageing, anxiety (such as performance anxiety), and a range of health problems that reduce blood to the brain like high blood pressure, stroke (kills brain cells), chronic pain, diabetes (high blood sugar), anemia (reduces oxygen to the brain), cardiac and respiratory disorders, insomnia (profound fatigue) and various deficiencies (for example B vitamins, selenium and protein).

In addition to memory loss (only when it is a major disruption of daily living) some warning signs are: difficulty performing familiar tasks; disorientation in time and place; poor or decreased judgement; a problem with language and abstract thinking; changes in mood, behaviour or personality; and continually misplacing things, something which tends to affect all ageing people. (Where are my glasses?)

It should be noted that some of these symptoms can be caused by other health problems such as a brain tumour, stress, depression, strokes, Parkinson's, multiple sclerosis, bipolar disease and hypothyroidism. Many dementias are progressive, so that symptoms start out slowly and gradually get worse. It is therefore important to get a medical assessment as soon as possible as there may be a treatable underlying condition rather than dementia.

In the end, most people with late-stage dementia die of a medical complication related to their dementia. For instance, a person may die from an infection like aspiration pneumonia, which occurs as a result of swallowing difficulties, or a person may die from a blood clot in the lung as a result of being immobile and bed-bound. When there are swallowing difficulties, poor eating and drinking lead to weight loss, dehydration and malnutrition, which further increases vulnerability to infection.

Last Days

When a person is told they have a terminal illness the next question is usually: "How long have I got?"

An attending professional will give an educated guess of perhaps weeks, months or even years, depending on the nature of the illness. However, they generally don't know the person very well, so it is hard to know when 'last' is actually last, except perhaps when it comes to the final few days. We are, after all, a unified combination of body, mind and spirit, and all three are involved even when the body is dying.

Some people just seem to hang on, perhaps until an event like a birthday occurs. Others, on whom health professionals have given up, have survived – which makes euthanasia a major problem. Also, with a limited life ahead, some change their priorities and go through a transformation.

Although suffering is very subjective, pain can be controlled and palliative care may be needed earlier on and not just for the last few days. In New Zealand such care can be provided at home and not just in a hospital.

A common misunderstanding is that palliative care hastens death when, in fact, its aim is simply to improve the quality of life. Often a person goes into a hospice near the end and are given enough medication to make them comfortable. When they shortly die it is not because of the medication but because they were already about to die. Although pain is part of dying, pain is not always inevitable, and alleviating drugs can reduce pain to a bit of discomfort. I used to believe that morphine is administered to hasten death. Not so. If a person is on morphine for two weeks it is hard to hasten death with it. Some people may believe that pain medications lead to addiction when in fact addiction or drug abuse is rare in such cases.

There are some well-defined stages a person may go through in their last days that are described below, but not everyone goes through them. However, knowing about them can help to allay some fears.

We find that being with a person, even in silence, is usually the best thing we can do, especially near the end, although some activities like looking at photographs can be helpful. Hearing is one of the last things to go, even if a person cannot respond, so we need to assume they can hear us. One telling sign is when a person says they are ready to go or says they are dying.

I now want to consider some of the things a caregiver might expect to happen near the end. The following has arisen mainly from notes I have taken from two webinars given by Dr Amanda

Landers of Nurse Maude Hospice and Otago Medical School. Information is also available on the internet.

Symptoms like restlessness, confusion, and agitation are common towards the end, and a patient may need anti-anxiety medication and/or a muscle relaxant. The patient may be experiencing emotional pain so it is helpful to check if they are frightened or worried about something; they need to be heard.

It is common for a patient to withdraw from people for several reasons. For example, too many people can be annoying and tiring for the patient who may need to rest, as it takes energy to concentrate. People, particularly children and/or grandchildren, may feel they need to keep talking. On the other hand, visitors don't always know what to talk about; just being there is important. However, as already mentioned, patients can also withdraw in preparation for leaving behind friends and loved ones.

A dying person who has found peace and acceptance in their death will have to separate themselves, step by step, from their environment, including their most loved ones. How can a person be ready to die if he or she continues to hold onto meaningful relationships rather than letting go? As an aside, I should mention that we do not need to protect children from the process of dying but we need to allow time for them to say goodbye and emphasise, if needed, that it is not their fault. We need to explain openly and honestly and allow for questions.

Towards the end various organs can be affected, depending of course on the nature of a person's illness. The brain becomes compromised through a lack of oxygen so drowsiness and fatigue is often present. It is very common for a patient to nod off in mid-sentence and they may have difficulty waking up. Communication with a patient can be awkward as they may have difficulty corresponding to voice and touch and in finding words. They may also delay in answering as they find it hard to find words, which is what I found with one of my dying friends. They may even speak to someone who is not there.

However, it is important to encourage the patient to talk if possible, even if messages have difficulty getting through. Such communication problems are amplified if the patient has a brain tumour which, in the earlier stages, can lead to a disconcerting personality change as well as their forgetting how to do basic things such as sitting down and walking. Swallowing can be difficult as it takes brain and muscle power to do this so there may be coughing, choking, loss of gag reflex, and the sound of throat secretions. Hearing these secretions is not necessarily cause for alarm as the patient may not even be aware of what is happening.

If the patient cannot swallow tablets, medication can be applied under the skin. Mouth care can be helpful such as cleaning using swabs, vaseline on the lips, and cleaning teeth. There may also be moaning and groaning that can be unsettling for the listener, but this may be due to the patient dreaming or trying to communicate, rather than due to pain. Patients can also have shuddering limbs, and the loss of reflexes in the legs and arms are additional signs that the end of life is near. A major problem in patient care is toileting because of incontinence. The patient experiences loss of sphincter control – a muscle which helps to control the doorway to the bladder. Muscular contraction is needed for a bowel movement so that this can also be compromised. There can be side issues with fungal infections and skin problems.

I have already referred to some breathing problems; supplying oxygen is not helpful. If the patient is coughing after food it is time to stop eating. With the gut, the patient's metabolic rate decreases, almost stopping, and the person can exist on very little food and fluid. This means that there is little fluid intake and a lack of appetite, so forced feeding and drinking are out of the question! Dehydration is not painful. In fact, IV fluids are not helpful as they can cause oedema (fluid retention). What is happening is that the gut can no longer process food, so the kidneys (the filtering system) shut down and brain euphoria takes away hunger and thirst, allowing the body to wind down. People with an advanced illness do not experience hunger and thirst as healthy people do.

We need to let the patient say what they need. The patient will of course lose weight, but not necessarily through loss of food, and this can be distressing as you see your loved one waste away. I found this difficult with the death of my first wife at 46 and others, even though that part of the dying process is normal.

I refer again to the lungs. What you hear can be very distressing even though the patient is comfortable. For example, breathing can be abnormal with apnoea or gasping (called agonal breathing), but the irregular breath will not generally be painful and the patient is usually unaware of their noisy breathing. If by chance the patient gets a chest infection antibiotics won't be helpful, and chest infection is often the mode of death. When the lungs begin to fail, a huge load is placed on the heart. The pulse can become rapid, and it can also become weak and irregular. There can also be a change in temperature with cool hands and feet, or the patient may have a drenching sweat. There is also less urine and it can be dark. However, if the pulse is strong, there are still hours before death.

Finally, a person may have terminal delirium, where there is a day-night reversal with sleeping in the daytime and waking at night. Frequently the person eventually relapses into a coma. Key signs of approaching death are the so-called death rattle due to a secretion build up in the back of the throat, a lack of a radial pulse (in the wrist), and a pale or greyish colour or mottling of the skin. Towards the end it can be very difficult to look after a patient, especially if the patient has dementia and loses connection with what is going on; they usually need to go into some kind of residential care. For terminal care a person might need to go into a hospice where they can get specialist medication at the end, though a reasonable percentage of people die at home.

Hospice Care

As hospices are charitable organizations, hospice care is available free of charge in New Zealand. Any patient over the age of eighteen with an active and advanced life-limiting disease – such as cancer, heart failure, motor-neuron disease or multiple sclerosis – may be referred for hospice support at some point in their illness. A referral is normally made by a person's own general practitioner or hospital doctor. A district nurse may also make a referral. In most areas people can also contact the hospice directly to discuss what support might be available.

People may be referred for hospice care as soon as a diagnosis is made, not just at the very end of life. Once a person's palliative care needs have been met they may be discharged from the service for the time being. Patients are often referred at a time when they are at the end of active treatment, and particularly if they have complex symptoms that require specialist management. However, they can be reassessed at any time after this if their condition changes.

A referral can be made even while a patient is undergoing treatment for an illness, not just at the very end of life, although such a referral usually occurs at a time when it is acknowledged the illness is incurable. Patients who are nearing the end may also want to discuss where they wish to die, so it is important they know of the additional support a hospice may be able to give them.

Hospices have available a team of district nurses and other health care professionals working alongside general practitioners. Trained hospital teams provide specialist health and social care, either in the home or in inpatient care.

Expert help and advice is available 24 hours a day, seven days a week. Hospice care has a unique whole-person approach which means physical, spiritual, emotional and social needs are equally important. A multidisciplinary team provides care for the person who is dying as well as for their families and friends, both before and after death.

2

AFTER THE FUNERAL

First Things First

Following a death a surviving partner or family members may still be numb from what has happened, but are carried along by the need to organize a funeral service and reception, as well as providing accommodation for visiting family members.

They may also be in denial over the death, which sees them through the early stages. This means friends may get the wrong idea at the time and think that the survivors have got over the loss very well and are doing fine. However, after a while the realisation sets in as to what has happened and that the one who has died has truly gone.

Although it might be difficult at the time, legal matters need to be attended to straight away, utilising the momentum of the funeral before feelings of loss and grief need attention.

If a funeral director is used, he or she will register the death with the registrar of Births, Deaths and Marriages, and will need to be given some personal information about the person who has died. Friends need to be informed. A checklist of organisations that need to be contacted is given below.

The assets of the dead person that are not jointly owned need to be immediately frozen until the will is finally executed (technically referred to as probate). However, a joint bank account may also be frozen before being transferred to the surviving partner. The same holds for joint assets that will eventually pass to the surviving owner and do not form part of the estate. It is, however, necessary to obtain a copy of the certified death certificate (ordered by toll free number 0800 22 52 52 within NZ) to give to the banks and any other institutions that may have jointly-held assets, with a request to transfer the assets to the surviving owner.

In the case of land owned jointly, it is necessary for the title to be transferred into the name of the surviving owner. The estate's lawyer will prepare this documentation and arrange signing and registration. The appointment of one or more executors was discussed in chapter one. They need to be granted so-called probate in court to be the will's executors. This process of probate can take some time, perhaps weeks, as things get sorted out.

The executor will need the following details:

- names and addresses of the beneficiaries;

- dates of birth of any beneficiaries under 20 years of age (anything left to beneficiaries under the age of 20 must be held in trust until their 20th birthday unless the will states otherwise);

- details of bank accounts, automatic payments, bonus bonds, investments, shares and debentures, unit trusts, mortgage investments, managed funds, KiwiSaver or other superannuation schemes, life insurance, any business interests, real property (residential home, investment property…), motor vehicles, jointly owned property, any liabilities, insurance policies (held for property, contents and motor vehicles), passport and driving licence;

- name of employer, details of any work-related superannuation scheme and any other employee benefits payable on the death of an employee. Also, all debts owed by the estate need to be paid, which the lawyer usually does when invoices are provided.

A funeral grant might be available from Work and Income, ACC, or medical insurance.

The executor will need to arrange for any life or funeral insurance to be paid out; check whether the deceased is owed any pay or superannuation from their workplace; cancel any bills or accounts under the deceased's name; cancel the passport (toll free 0800 22 50 50, NZ only), and cancel any driver's licence (contact NZTA, 0800 822 422, NZ only).

The Inland Revenue Department should be contacted if the deceased had a student loan, paid or received child support, had a KiwiSaver account, or ran a business. A final tax return will need to be made and the IRD will explain what information is needed. Any estate income still being received by the dead person's estate should be included. Work and Income need to be contacted if the person who died was being paid a benefit such as NZ Super (pension), Veteran's Pension (under 65, 0800 559 009; over 65, 0800 552 002), or Government Super. Any tax or financial issues are required to be sorted before the will is executed.

In many cases executors are also named as trustees. Duties and responsibilities of executors and trustees are very similar, with the difference being that the executor's role finishes when the will is finalized, with all distributions made to adult beneficiaries and all expenses/tax have been paid. The trustee's role may continue for some time if trusts have been set up. Executors will continue as trustees if money is held for under-age beneficiaries.

New Zealand law, which differs from other countries, does allow some people to make claims against an estate after the will-maker has died. This may mean the court will override the will to some extent. Unfortunately, the possibility that a claim might be made means it is not always possible to distribute the estate proceeds immediately.

Grief

Much of what follows in the next section is based on Seber (2013: chapter 11.)

In talking about grief I use the personal pronoun 'you' even though others may be involved. The first thing that comes up is whether you wish to view the body or not.

Generally speaking, it is a good idea to view the body, perhaps with suitable company, say goodbye, and thus have some closure. This is particularly the case if you weren't there at the end. However, if you were there at the end you may not feel it necessary. On the other hand, if your loved one dies at home you may wish to keep the body there for an appropriate time. In some cultures, viewing the body and paying last respects is part of the normal grieving process. For me, the most striking observation about viewing a dead body is that you are aware that the person is gone and that only a physical shell remains.

It has been said that it takes two years to get over a major loss, but I don't believe it is a good idea to use such a statistic. Everybody is different about how they process grief, even though there are some stages of grief people can go through.

There is no right or wrong way for you to grieve, or an appropriate length of time for grieving. You need to give yourself permission to grieve in your own way and according to your own schedule. There is freedom in giving yourself permission to grieve. If death came after a long illness, and you are left exhausted and too numb to grieve, you may initially feel guilty that you are relieved it is finally over. I have found personally that a long illness does help to prepare you for the end as you have already done some of your grieving over that time, and made preparations as described in the previous chapter.

It is important to remember that grief is not something that needs fixing or curing! It is not an illness nor a psychological problem. Grief is what you experience as you go through the process of grieving.

In fact, the best thing you can do with grief is grieve! Paradoxically, when we hurt the most we are perhaps doing the best job with our grief. We don't control grief. We can only experience it and let it roll over us, wave after wave. You might find that mental confusion reigns and your mind whirls with questions such as: "How long will I hurt like this?"

Strong feelings of grief can reoccur over a lifetime; they are not continuous after an initial period of the first few days or weeks. Grief generally gets worse for a time as it goes deeper and the full impact of the loss is felt, but in time the waves do become less frequent and less overwhelming. Sometimes there will be reminders and triggers that bring another wave, such as holidays, anniversaries, music, and night time. A sight, sound, smell or memory may bring an acute awareness of the deceased person to mind and trigger a flood of tears.

A lot of the time there is no explanation for the wave, and when a wave comes you may feel that you have made no progress. However, it does provide an opportunity for further growth and it helps to give yourself permission to let the tears flow freely.

You need to acknowledge how you feel and act according to your feelings, not according to what you or others think you should feel. You might find writing a letter or letters to the deceased can help you to express your feelings and take care of unfinished business. In the end, suffering is a mystery that you may find difficult to deal with because there can be many unanswered questions. How you deal with these may depend on how you see the spiritual side of life. You may struggle with your spirituality and reassess your beliefs.

As mentioned in the previous section, there is a lot that has to be done initially, but you do need to take your time over making decisions like what to do with a loved one's belongings (clothing, books, collections), whether you should change your living conditions and perhaps move (which is traumatic just on its own), or correspond with friends and family via possible thankyou letters.

You may find there is a huge void in your life, once filled by caring for your loved one, and this can affect decision making. For example, if you eventually have to go back to work, when is a good time to do this? Often people can return to work soon after a death, but may need time off later when reality sets in and the crash comes. It might be an idea to visit the workplace before returning to work, if only to see the manager or chat with colleagues to break the ice. Being part-time for a couple of weeks may suit some people but not others, though it will depend on the type of work.

Stages of Grief

Some people go through various stages when they grieve, and a popular version of this (Kübler-Ross, 1978) described the stages after the initial shock as denial, anger, bargaining, depression, and acceptance. Initially these stages referred to someone who was dying, and then they came to be applied to the process after death.

Other lists are available such as that of Westberg (1962) who has a ten-stage list: shock, emotion, depression and loneliness; physical symptoms of stress; panic (because we can't get the loss out of our mind); guilt (because of wrongs and/or unfinished business); anger (at God or caregivers for allowing the death); resistance (we don't want to get back into life again as we don't want to minimise the loss, or because life is too painful); hope (which slowly filters through); and affirmation of reality (and our spirituality). Do you identify with any of these?

There is general agreement that shock and a temporary escape from reality is the first stage, and you might find that initially you feel numb and on auto-pilot. This contributes to being able to get through the funeral and related activities. If you are at this stage I would encourage you to carry on your usual activities as much as possible. Doing nothing is not going to help.

Westberg has the analogy of recovery from surgery where they get you moving almost straight away, as it speeds up recovery. In fact, if you stand up in hospital they may pinch your bed!

One stage a person may go through is anger. You may be angry with your loved one for dying and leaving you like that. If your loved one committed suicide you may be angry that he or she took the easy way out and left you to clear up afterwards. You may be angry with God for allowing the death to happen, or angry with the church for not being there when it mattered most, or angry with the way the funeral was conducted. If, after an inquest, it turned out that the death was caused by negligence (by a doctor or hospital, for example) then you may be angry with the people who were negligent.

You may be angry with your partner over the death of a child. Friends may say the wrong things and you may get angry with them and their good intentions and advice. You may be angry with yourself, and what sometimes comes to mind is the phrase, "if only I…" You can get obsessed with the idea that you might have contributed in some way to the death, or have regrets over unfinished business.

There is always unfinished business and we have to accept this. If the death was not sudden should we have talked about death at the time, or was it better to just leave things be and not say our final goodbyes? We make our decision at the time and accept the fact that it was the best we could do under the circumstances.

A third stage might be anxiety. Strategies for coping with this might include avoiding changes, not thinking about too many things at once, and not overplanning your day. Allow plenty of 'time out'. Don't force yourself to do something when you cannot concentrate, though some kind of distraction can be helpful, such as walking, listening to music, or engaging in a hobby.

Depression is usually present at some stage in the grief process. You need to remember that there is no hard and fast list of stages that you will go through. In fact, some people may go backwards or forwards through some stages.

Moving On

I have mentioned just three possible stages of grief, and others were referred to above. Although such lists of stages make good sense and can be helpful, I shall now discuss the grieving process more fully from the point of view of what might need to happen (Attig,1996).

One problem is that grieving people can act better than they really are and hide their pain from others. However, I guess one thing you want is for people to understand you and appreciate something of what you have been through, people who will listen patiently to the details of your stories of life with the dead person, the events surrounding the death, and your life now. No story of loss replicates any other, and you want people to understand how life-shattering the death is. It does not help if a person says they know how you feel as you want them to respect the uniqueness of your experience and hear all the details of the challenges you are facing in every avenue of your life. We all need someone we can talk to honestly.

Although no one fully understands how you feel, as your pain is unique, talking at least helps you to recognise that you are no longer alone in your pain. It helps to legitimise your feelings and enables you to move on. You need safe people who will listen, instead of trying to explain things away or offer advice. Talking helps us release our feelings and often give us insight. It's rather like talking about a problem which helps us see a solution. You may need to tell the story over and over again until you believe that the story has actually been heard. It may sound like a cracked record played repeatedly to the outsider, but when heard by an understanding friend it brings healing.

Bereavement is a choiceless event over which you have little or no control, and you may have no control over the havoc it brings into your life. Although grief is an emotion you may experience as overwhelming, it is a coping process that is not choiceless but involves active participation in addressing an environment without the loved one; a process of accepting the reality of the loss and relearning the world again.

A metaphor I find helpful is that grief is a like a black cloud over the whole sky. In time, the cloud shrinks and blue sky, white clouds, and birds begin to appear around the edges until eventually the black cloud is small and swamped in light and colour. This cloud may not completely disappear but simply becomes part of the landscape of life. For many people the pain of grief never completely goes, but it is surrounded by good things. One guideline for recovery from grief is when you are able to think of the deceased person without pain. There will always be sadness in losing a loved one, but it won't have the physical manifestations that go with intense grief. Rituals are important, such as grave visiting, especially during the initial months and on special occasions such as birthdays.

The final stage of recovery might be described as reconstruction; when you decide to move on with your life and begin again. There will be moments when you begin to feel normal again! Letting go can be difficult, and an important question to ask is this: what is an appropriate connection between you and the death of your loved one?

In the past there has been a tendency to tell bereaved people to sever their relationship with the deceased and move on; maintaining a bond with the deceased can be regarded as symptomatic of psychological problems. This kind of advice is no longer considered appropriate as we should not completely let go of our loved one. Referring to Attig (1996: 174-175), you don't need to break your bonds with the deceased, but instead redefine the nature of those bonds and their place in your life. You can continue to love the person, but in a different way by letting go and letting be.

You may need to forgive any of their shortcomings or failings. There is a need to continue to love and cherish the stories of your loved one and to care about the things he or she cared about. You can, for example, collect material about the deceased, such as creating scrapbooks, photo albums, and/or a biographical journal.

In the recovery process, there will also be times when you experience triggers and the tears flow. You need to give yourself permission to let them flow freely. There is freedom in giving ourselves permission to grieve. You also need the freedom to let yourself laugh again, love again, and live again. You don't need to live your life according to what you think your departed loved one would want; you need to give yourself freedom to change traditions, if necessary.

Two extreme reactions to avoid are either building a wall and shutting yourself off from social activity, or trying to kill the pain by an incessant round of social activity. Something you might need to do is learn some new skills and move out of a traditional role. For example, a woman might need to take the car for a service and learn to do odd fix-it jobs around the house, while a man might need to shop, cook, buy clothes (say, for children), and perhaps learn sewing. Also, your friends may change. Some old friends may avoid you as they don't know what to say, or you may feel uncomfortable with the old crowd who don't really appreciate how you feel.

Memories also change. At first they are very painful, but eventually they can become something to embrace. Rituals can be helpful, like visiting a grave and perhaps leaving some flowers. A year after my present wife's mother died, the family met around her grave and shared stories. They then all went out to lunch to celebrate her life. There is no right or wrong way of doing this kind of thing, but it may be helpful to have some sort of get-together in a family situation.

Children's Grief

I want to speak to those whose children have also suffered the loss of a family member. How children respond to grief depends on their age, their relationship with the one who has died, and their type of attachment.

Up to the age of five, children do not understand the full meaning of the word 'death' and do not appreciate that death is final. They see things concretely, so abstract explanations should be avoided. Explanations need to be simple such as, "Usually when we get sick we get better, but Grandpa died because he was very, very, very sick and his body was unable to go on living so it stopped." Euphemisms like saying that the dead person is asleep or gone on a long journey may be taken literally, especially as young children are very sensitive to separations. However, there is no reason to doubt that they react strongly to loss even though they may not have the language to explain their feelings.

From five to ten, children begin to understand that death is irreversible and final, and at around seven begin to realise that death is unavoidable and universal. They are still concrete in their thinking and their understanding of the causes of death, so they are helped by concrete expressions of grief such as memorial acts and rituals.

From ten through adolescence a child's concept of death becomes more abstract, though concrete memorial acts remain important. Several years ago I heard the story of a twelve-year-old boy who, after the funeral for his sixteen-year-old sister, organised the flowers that came to the house along either side of the front entrance and front hall as a memorial.

It is important to keep reminders of the dead person present, and look at albums and photographs. Children might want to express how they feel in different ways about the deceased person, such as producing a scrapbook of memories using drawings, pictures, press cuttings, photos, and their own and perhaps others' writings, and should be helped to do so. It is also helpful to create and notice opportunities to remember and celebrate the deceased person, such as birthdays and anniversaries. Teenagers can find it difficult to reconcile their desire to be with the family with their drive for autonomy, peer acceptance, and social activities.

Bereaved parents need to be aware of the effect that death has on their children. Children grieve differently from adults and we cannot view their grieving through adult eyes. My boys were eleven and fourteen when my first wife died. In retrospect I recognise that personal grief can stop you from fully appreciating the grief of your children. Often their grief goes unacknowledged, even unrecognised.

Children need to be allowed to grieve as children. For example, children do not grieve continuously but take breaks; they may delay their grief or mix it with play (which can be disconcerting for adults). Children need to be kept informed of what is going on, in words they can understand, so that surprises are minimised. As with adults, every child grieves differently. Here are some common immediate reactions.

- Shock and disbelief. They may refuse to accept the death, and parents can be surprised that their children do not react more than they do.

- Dismay and protest. They cry a lot and initially seem inconsolable.

- Apathy and stunned feelings.

- Continuation of usual activities. This can be unsettling for parents, but it is a protection mechanism for the child.

Children need to know that they will be cared for and perhaps reassured that they were not to blame for what happened, and that the person did not want to leave them.

As with adults, children can have a wide range of grief reactions. For example: anxiety – such as fear of losing the other parent or dying themselves – vivid memories (unwelcome repeated thoughts and images); sleep difficulties (fear of bad dreams); sadness and longing (searching for the lost one); anger and acting out (anger at God, adults, self, and even the dead person for allowing it to happen); guilt, self-reproach, and shame (blaming themselves for their past behaviour); school problems (concentration problems); and physical complaints (for example, stomach problems).

As a defence mechanism children may try to keep the event at a distance until they slowly get used to the idea. It is important that a child is not forced into a surrogate parent role for the remaining partner. Like adults, sudden death creates other problems for a child, for there isn't time to say goodbye. In particular, suicide creates problems for both adults and children.

How adults handle death has a big impact on the children, particularly if the children are not updated as to what is going on. It is not helpful if children are excluded from the adult world in various ways such as preventing them from seeing the dead person if they want to (though they need to be properly prepared by having all the details of the body and room described beforehand), or taking part in the funeral (or any other rituals such as visiting the grave), or even seeing the adults' reactions. A difficult situation can be made worse for them. If they see adults in tears they may feel less disturbed about how they feel.

By discussing the death openly and sensitively the child can learn to do the same. The children also need structure in their lives so that the usual routines can be maintained. They may have difficulty in sorting out what their friends can be told or dealing with the discomfort that others have with the death.

It can be particularly difficult for a child whose parent has committed suicide. The child needs to realise that they were not to blame and that the person did not want to leave them. They will need to explore the reasons for the suicide and their feelings about it. If the suicide was due to mental illness they may be afraid it will happen to them. On the other hand, they may feel upset at the apparent lack of care or love shown by the bereaved that allowed them to ignore the child's need by dying.

Counselling will be particularly helpful for a child bereaved because of trauma from suicide or murder, or for a child having witnessed a death. A child may need professional help if there is excessive crying for long periods, frequent temper tantrums, nightmares and sleep disturbances, extreme changes in behaviour, headaches or other physical complaints. Other things to look for are changes in school performance, general apathy and withdrawal with a loss of interest in friends and previously enjoyed activities, and a negative outlook about the future.

Let us not forget any pets involved as they may seem to grieve and need to be talked to and comforted. There are many stories about the responses to death of dogs and cats, and these animals seem to go through a grieving process when their master dies.

Suicide and Sudden Death

People who have lost a loved one through suicide, especially parents losing a child, face a difficult grief journey. They may be overwhelmed by a sense of shock and horror at the suicide and this may be compounded by the way it was carried out. It is not uncommon to experience feelings of guilt and shame for not anticipating or even preventing what happened. You may be angry with the person for taking the easy way out and leaving you to cope with the trauma, problems and unfinished business left behind. You may also feel that others blame you for the suicide, especially if it's a child or teenager, and feel stigmatised by it. Perhaps the cause of death was not recorded accurately.

If you don't know anyone who has faced the same situation, you may feel very isolated; support groups can be helpful here. Any guilt, or rage, needs to be acknowledged, listened to empathetically, and normalised. Two big questions that you might face are "Why has this happened?" and "How can I make sense of this?" It can be helpful to try to find some meaning in the death, though this can be very difficult and may take some time.

Sometimes a family creates a myth about what really happened. They may, for example, describe the death as accidental with no one being allowed to challenge the belief. The subject may not even be allowed to be discussed. Such distorted thinking is not productive in the long run. Previous patterns of family communication may no longer work as the grief is so profound. Rituals can be very helpful, using such things as food, water, candles, music, fire, paper, and fragrance.

Although suicide is a sudden death, there are other examples when a death occurs without warning – an accident, natural disaster, heart attack or homicide. In these cases, the survivor will usually have a sense of unreality about the loss and, as with a suicide, there can be strong feelings of guilt, anger and a sense of helplessness.

Unfinished business is of special concern and there is often a strong desire to blame someone for the death. There may also be legal and medical ramifications when some form of malpractice, such as not having proper safety standards, is involved; this can lead to a protracted investigation. Viewing the body of the deceased may help a survivor actualise the loss, and keep him/her focused on the death rather than on the circumstances of the death. That is one reason why, for many people, it is important to retrieve the body, if possible.

Death of a Child

The death of a child is extremely traumatic, and is generally regarded as the most difficult loss to bear, especially if it's an only child. It is very hard to let the child go after death, and for some people it's almost impossible. Not only is the child lost, but also all the potential that the child might have is lost too. This loss of a potential future can be acutely felt, especially at special times such an anniversary of the loss, and can haunt parents for the rest of their lives. Writing a letter to the child can help the healing.

Losing a child through cot death (SIDS – Sudden Infant Death Syndrome) or a miscarriage can also be devastating. Cot death is very distressing as it occurs without warning and for no apparent reason. Guilt is usually keenly felt by the parents, with sometimes irrational blaming between spouses. Older siblings may have resented the arrival of the baby and may now experience guilt and remorse. Any grandparents may need support. There can also be a communication breakdown between husband and wife, especially as their responses to grief may be very different. Sexual relations may be suspended because of the fear of pregnancy and a repeat of the experience. The death of one's child is so unsettling because it is contrary to the accepted idea that children live on after us. It may also involve the aspect that the child will not be there to support the parent(s) in old age.

Parents can experience various types of guilt (Miles and Demi, 1991).

- Cultural guilt. Society expects parents to look after their children.

- Causal guilt. This can arise if there was any real or perceived negligence, or if the death was due to some inherited problem.

- Moral guilt. The death may be seen as a punishment for some previous misdemeanor, such as an abortion.

- Survival guilt. The question asked , "Why am I alive and not my child?" This is particularly relevant if the family has had an accident, with the child dying and the parents surviving.

- Recovery guilt. If I move on happily with my life, I am dishonouring the memory of my dead child.

Stillborn Child

It is recommended that a stillborn child be named, if that hasn't already happened, so that the child becomes part of the family.

There seems to be a consensus in studies of stillbirths that it is helpful for parents to see or hold their baby (or at least have the option of doing so) if it is possible. A photograph or any memorabilia may also be helpful. Clearly, the major part of the attachment process is completed before birth, thus highlighting the pain of the loss. Therefore, it is important to realise that the grieving process has similar features to that experienced in losing a spouse, even though it is more a loss of an anticipated future. A mother has to cope with breast milk, for example, as well as other hormonal changes. There will also be other reminders like baby clothes, a cot, and even a room especially prepared as a nursery.

A miscarriage or stillbirth has a heightened dimension of loneliness as only the mother knew and bonded with the child at the moment of conception. It is can also be a loss for the father, though he may not appreciate the depth of the loss for the mother if there is no physical bonding for him during pregnancy. Mothers often remember the specific details surrounding the loss for many years, and may be angry with the medical caregivers at the time, even blaming them for lack of care. Typical grief symptoms can include emptiness, body tension, sadness, anger, guilt, depression, sense of failure, preoccupation with thoughts of the baby, having a desire to be left alone, or not wanting to be alone.

Miscarriage

In the case of a miscarriage, grief is complex as the parents suffer from the effects of a birth and a death without usually having a funeral or a baby to bury. Because there is no tangible evidence of the death people generally don't know how to respond and may be unaware of the grief. In fact, the death may be minimised, especially if it occurred early in the pregnancy. It is the strength of the bond and not the length of the pregnancy that determines the depths of a mother's grief. Also, the hormonal after-effects of a pregnancy don't disappear immediately after the loss. The death can have an additional impact if it is the first pregnancy, and can also raise questions like, "Will I ever be a mother?" or "Can I trust my body?" or "Did I do something wrong?"

The extent of the grief will depend on many factors such as the hopes and expectations of the pregnancy. For example, the pregnancy may have been a replacement for former losses so that such past losses may compound the present loss. The marriage might have been shaky and the pregnancy might have provided the couple with hope for the future of their marriage. With the loss, a woman may feel pressured by herself or others to try to get pregnant again quickly.

There may also be an element of self-blame ("Was there something I shouldn't have done?") and some blame may be directed toward the husband. The loss can therefore cause distance and communication problems between husband and wife. The husband needs to be especially sensitive to his wife's needs at this time. Friends may not be very helpful; any inappropriate comments need to be ignored.

Other Siblings

At such a time, other siblings should not be forgotten as they will be aware that something is not right with their parents. They need adequate information even though the loss from a miscarriage is invisible, as they may blame the loss on their parents, on themselves, or wonder about their own safety. Also, some aftercare in hospital for the mother might be needed.

Children need to know that a miscarriage is a common and normal experience, and need to be kept informed so that they don't feel left out or confused. If there is a keepsake box the children might like to contribute something too as a memento, or help plant a tree. They need to know how a parent is feeling and that it is okay to cry. What the child needs to be told will depend on the age of the child. It is important that the child does not becomes a substitute for the lost child.

Conclusion

Although I have considered a number of ways of how the loss of a person can occur, there will be some people who don't fit in with the above descriptions. For example, refugees may have to deal not only with lost loved ones or friends, but other losses such as loss of possessions, loss of country, and even loss of identity.

It is hoped that the above comments are useful in more general situations. Any kind of loss involves grief, and if not dealt with it can compound with other losses. However, if we lose a loved one we can rest in the hope that eventually we will be able to move on.

REFERENCES

Attig, T. (1996). *How We Grieve: Relearning the World.* Oxford University Press, New York.

Cabot, S. (2005). *Alzheimer's: What You Must Know to Protect Your Brain.* Glendale, AZ, U.S: SCB Inc.

Kübler-Ross, E. (1978). *On Death and Dying.* Routledge, London.

Miles, M.S. and Demi, A.S. (1991). *A comparison of guilt in bereaved parents whose children died by suicide, accident, or chronic disease.* Omega, 24, 203– 215.

Seber, G.A.F. (2013). *Counseling Issues: A Handbook for Counselors and Psychotherapists.* Bloomington, IN, U.S: Xlibris.

Westerberg, G.E. (1962). *Good Grief: A Constructive Approach to the Problem of Loss.* Augustana Press, Rock Island, IL. (This book has since been reprinted many times by a variety of publishers, using a different number of pages, sometimes under the title of just *Good Grief.*)